THE LIES THEY TOLD

I Found Out That My Mother Is My Sister

TRINA DORSEY THOMPSON

ISBN: 979-8-9914835-0-6

Published by: POP Power Of Purpose Publishing

Www.PopPublishing.com
Atlanta, Ga. 30326

Disclaimer:

CONTENT WARNING: This book contains sexual and graphic content which may be offensive to some readers

The thoughts, actions, and or beliefs of characters in this book are from the personal experience of author(s) and some names and locations may have been changed to protect characters.

Although the author has made every effort to ensure that the information in this book was correct at press time, the author does not assume and hereby disclaims any liability to any party for any loss, damage, or disruption caused by errors or omissions, whether such errors or omissions result from negligence.

Dedication

To my beloved mother, Patrica Thompson for her unwavering strength and courage—together, we broke the chains of generational curses and built a new legacy. To my precious children, family, and dear friends, thank you for your love, faith, and support that lifted me when I needed it most. And above all, I give my deepest gratitude to God, who granted me the resilience, vision, and grace to bring this book to life. Without each of you, this journey would not have been possible. This work is for all of us—a testament to healing, hope, and unbreakable bonds

Watch Family Matters~ Healing through family trauma

Trina's new talk show brings hope while shedding light on family matters while healing through family trauma

www.ThePopTelevisionNetwork.com

Ready To Write And Publish Your Book?

Mention *Trina* for discount

www.IamReadyToWrite.com (free consultation)

www.PopPublishing.com

Get The Course That Will Help You To Finally Write That Book!

www.AuthorMastery.com

Use Promo Code Trina for discount

Table of Contents

When I was a young girl, I grew up thinking my grandparents were my parents. Then I found out that my family kept secrets, and everything changed when I turned ten. That's when the whispers started, the little hints that something wasn't quite right.

One summer afternoon, I overheard a conversation that shattered my world. My family was full of secrets—big ones. I learned that my mother had been put in a state school for youth with mild disabilities when she was just sixteen, right after I was born. And then came the truth that turned my life upside down: my grandfather was my father.

I felt the ground shift beneath me, a jolt of confusion and betrayal. The family I thought I knew was a façade, hiding the darkness of our past. My mother's silence echoed loudly, and I was left grappling with questions that had no easy answers. Who was I really? What did it mean to have a mother who was also my sister?

From that moment, I knew I had to dig deeper, to uncover the tangled web of my family's history. I was determined to find the truth, no matter how painful it might be.

How It All Began

My name is Trina Dorsey Thompson. I was born on August 15, 1975, to a woman named Patricia Ann Thompson. Growing up, I lived with my grandparents, convinced they were my parents. It wasn't until I was older that I discovered the truth: my grandmother was my biological grandmother, and my grandfather was both my grandfather and my father. That twisted reality set off the biggest struggle of my life—an all-consuming search for identity amidst a haze of lies and secrets.

My mother was the youngest of eight, the last in a long line of daughters. By the time they all hit sixteen, they were practically married off, one by one, like livestock at a market. But my mother? She didn't show up for her wedding. That act of defiance would become a pivotal moment that rippled through our family like a stone tossed into still water.

Let me take you down this journey.

I remember that sweltering summer day in 1980 like it was yesterday. My grandmother was hosting one of her legendary card game suppers—tables piled high with plates of gumbo and cornbread, the air thick with laughter and smoke from hand-rolled cigarettes. Family and friends crowded around, voices rising and falling like a jazz tune, the clatter of cards echoing off the walls of our cramped apartment.

But then it all turned chaotic. An argument erupted between my grandfather and my uncle's girlfriend, her voice cutting through the laughter like a knife. "Y'all need to tell Trina the truth about her grandfather and her mom!"

The room went silent, the laughter replaced by a heavy tension that could suffocate. My grandfather, known for his explosive temper and violent history, was a powder keg waiting to blow. He came stomping down the stairs, gun in hand, and before I knew it, he fired a shot into the air. People scattered, chairs flew, and the air filled with screams as they bolted for the door.

I stood frozen, my heart pounding. The whispers I had heard—rumors about my grandfather—suddenly came crashing down around me. Kids at school teased me, calling him my father, but I never understood the weight of those words until now. That night, the truth clawed its way into my consciousness, and I knew

I couldn't unhear what I had just heard. I was determined to dig deeper, no matter how painful the truth might be.

THE LIES AND THE COVER-UP

I grew up in the Calliope, a low-income housing project in the heart of New Orleans. Life there was raw, gritty, and bursting with vibrancy. It was a world where laughter and gunshots often shared the same breath, where survival was an art form, and love could be both a refuge and a weapon. My grandparents, though illiterate, were strong figures—my grandfather could build anything with his hands, while my grandmother obeyed his very word.

They had their secrets, and I often wondered if their fierce protection was laced with guilt for what they hid. They spoiled me, draping me in the finest clothes, which only fueled the envy that simmered among my aunts.

Let me break down the family dynamic.

Uncle # 1? He was a ghost in our lives, always keeping his distance. His last name was different—, a painful reminder of my grandfather's affair that he was having with my grandmother. Yes, when my grandmother had my uncle she was my grandfather's mistress. It wasn't until his first wife passed away that he married my grandmother, and because she had him before they were married, my grandfather would not allow him to carry his last name I'm assuming. Rumors were that he did not believe that my uncle was his son.

Uncles #2 and # 3? Gone too soon, snuffed out by car accidents that left nothing but memories in their wake. Uncle #3 had a daughter the family called Rabbit. We were a couple months apart, both born in 1975 with me being the oldest. We were no older than 6 or 7 years old when her father, my uncle passed away. My uncle's wife made sure me and Rabbit kept a close relationship. She grew up in the Magnolia projects. I can remember the times I was allowed to spend the weekends there; me and Rabbit were always into something. We even had to go to summer school together. When her mom moved her away I felt like I had lost my best friend. We managed to keep in touch and she is still one of my favorite cousins.

Uncle # 4 lived with us, but unfortunately he never had any kids and never married. He was a handyman with a heart as big as the bayou, yet a drug addiction that ebbed and flowed like the

Mississippi. Despite our occasional clashes, he loved fiercely and would do anything for his family. The only big brother I knew.

Aunt #1, Maggie was my safe haven. Her home was a warm embrace, a gathering spot where everyone felt welcome. She cooked like a chef at a five-star restaurant and treated me like gold, offering a love I desperately craved.

But my other aunts? They were a different story. Auntie # 2 had ice in her veins; our connection felt strained, riddled with hurtful truths she'd spill when the whiskey flowed too freely. Auntie # 3 was a whirlwind of chaos, blaming me for family feuds I never caused. It was like being a piñata in a room full of blindfolded relatives—every swing was random, but the hurt was always real.

Then there were my great aunts, four sisters, who were my grandmother's sisters, who had their own unique vibes. One was strict, another nurturing, while another was a ball of joy. They had their battles but forged an unbreakable bond that I loved, and longed to emulate.

As the years passed, I could feel the truth gnawing at me. I couldn't escape the whispers, the taunts, or the shadow of my grandfather's legacy. I watched my family navigate their pain and secrets, each of us burdened by our own history.

In this tangled web, I found my voice—I needed to unravel this mess, not just for myself, but for my mother, who had been silenced for far too long.

And so, my journey began, driven by a relentless pursuit of truth, healing, and justice in a world that often felt devoid of both. I was determined to piece together my family's story, no matter how ugly it might get, because at the end of the day, the truth was the only thing that could set me free.

Growing up, my mama was not in the home. I didn't really know her; she was more like a shadow haunting my childhood. I was raised by my grandparents while she was locked away, and they never bothered to tell me the truth until I was ten. By then, the whispers in the neighborhood had already painted a picture of confusion and pain. Every weekend, they would take me to see this woman, who at the time, I did not know.

My grandparents would drive me to that place—a large, cold building that felt more like a prison than a home. My heart raced every time we went; something in me sensed that I was walking into a nightmare.

When I confronted my grandmother about the rumors, it felt like I was lifting a rock to find a nest of snakes. Secrets wrapped around my family like a noose. I asked why everyone knew about my mama's struggles—why she was locked up—and the only answer

I got was silence. "Just be quiet," they said, but I couldn't stop the questions from spilling out.

I heard stories of my mama getting into drugs and the horror that came with it, but the real betrayal came when I learned how she was mistreated. My head spun with confusion; if everyone knew, why was no one held accountable? One of my great aunts, my grandmother's sister painted a different picture of my mama—a sweet girl, caught in a storm she couldn't control. That was the truth I held onto.

The Visits

Every visit during my childhood to that facility felt like stepping into a horror movie. The wild-eyed folks screaming and running made me question my own sanity. My childhood was taken away from me. I would see my mama, but it felt like I was meeting a stranger. She called my grandfather "Uncle J " and would barely acknowledge my presence. I was left feeling abandoned, as if I didn't matter at all.

Then came the day everything changed. My mama was allowed to come home on a visit. I must have been around 7 or 8 years old. I was scared and excited at the same time. I still didn't know who she was but for some reason I had some type of attachment to her. I felt deep inside that I should know who she was but didn't want to. I had so many mixed emotions.

Then, my mama snapped, and chaos erupted. She ran out of the house and down the street. My uncles chased her down, and I watched in horror as they restrained her and dragged her back. After that, the home visits stopped altogether. I lost any chance to connect with the woman who was supposed to be my mother on a deeper level as a kid.

The Truth

The dread in my gut grew heavier every time they said we were going to see this woman. I was sick of the lies, sick of feeling like I was caught in someone else's story. Finally, my grandmother sat me down and revealed the truth: "The lady we visit? That's your mother." Just like that, my world shattered again.

The layers of lies unraveled, and I learned my mama had been a victim of unimaginable horror. I felt like I was carrying the weight of the world on my shoulders, all because I wanted to understand who I was.

My Other Dad

Then to top it all off as if I wasn't confused enough, steps in Anthony; my other dad. Anthony was the guy that my mom was dating when she got pregnant with me. They were high school sweethearts. They had planned to marry in 1975 but my mom stood him up at the altar. Yep, you heard right! It's all a whirlwind.

Anthony was a short, dark-skinned man from the 9th ward. He brought money every weekend and filled in the blanks I didn't even know existed. I'd spend weekends at his house, where he'd share stories about my mama and the love they once had. I felt a glimmer of hope, but the reality was different. I asked my grandparents, why would this man claim to be my dad when I already had a dad? They would just say that he was your mother's true love and he just wanted to step in and help raise you out of the goodness of his heart. A convenient scapegoat if you ask me. By him coming around, I think that my grandparents hoped that it would silence all of the rumors. A man stepping in to be my dad meant that my grandfather couldn't be my father, right?

As I got older, at around 12 years old, my dad started dating Miss Linda, a Pentecostal lady who had strict rules about how I should dress. I didn't like the fact that she told me how to dress, and she started taking me to church. I found solace in their church until my grandparents found out. They shut that door fast, just like they had done with so many others.

Then came the news that Anthony and Linda were moving to California. Linda felt that if my dad was truly my father, why would he need to keep getting permission from my grandparents about my well being? They decided to get a DNA test, I felt the ground shift beneath me. I was ready to know the truth, yet terrified at the same time. I knew that once it was revealed that he wasn't my father, he would be asked to leave my life for good. Then the truth,

I wasn't his child *was* revealed, and that revelation hit me like a ton of bricks. I can remember the day that Anthony came to the house in the U-Haul. My grandfather with his violent temper exploded on him. I ran after the U-Haul, screaming, "Don't leave me!" But my granddaddy's anger silenced my pleas.

The last I heard from Anthony was a letter. He explained that he wanted to stay around to give me the dad that I never had. It was important to him that he honor my mom. What a good and stand up dude! I was so sad, yet grateful at the same time. At least for a while I had the experience of having *a real dad*. I will always cherish that. He had a son now, named James Andrews, and had changed his own name. Just like that, I lost the only father figure I had ever known.

The Pain

That loss deepened my abandonment issues. If Anthony wasn't my dad, then who was? Depression settled in, feeding off the trauma I had endured. The abuse from my cousins haunted me, a dark secret I buried deep. Who would believe me? I swallowed it all, hiding my pain behind a mask of normalcy.

My family wore their dysfunction like a badge of honor, making it feel normal. They walked around as if everything was okay while I felt like a stranger in my own skin. I had nightmares about my mama's screams, and I just wanted to be loved. I didn't know much about my mama, but one thing I do know is that she didn't deserve the hand that she was dealt. I could see her life so vividly, it played out like a movie in my head over and over again. Her screams, her yelling "NO!" plagued me and I couldn't let her go. I knew that when the time came, I would fight for her with every inch of my being, and not stop until she was free!

As I grew, my anger toward my family boiled over. My grandfather's drinking left scars on our family dynamics, and my grandmother turned a blind eye. I felt like an outcast, but every summer I escaped to Baton Rouge, where my grandmother's sister offered me a glimmer of hope. She taught me to pray and shared stories that connected the broken pieces of my family. I thank GOD for this woman! She shared the stories of how everyone on my grandmother's side did not like my grandfather. He was dating their older sister first, then once my grandfather found out that he could not manipulate her, he went on to her younger sister: my grandmother. Twisted I know!

She also shared how my grandfather had a violent temper. Then, about how he had gotten into some trouble when he was younger and his brothers put him in the trunk of a car and drove him to New Orleans.

I later found out that my grandfather and his brothers were all pedophiles. That curse more than likely carried from generation to generation.

She also started sharing the story about uncle # 1 and how he was conceived. My grandmother was my grandfather's mistress and did not marry her until his first wife died. Uncle #1 was conceived before they were married and carried my grandmother's maiden name. It was never changed because my grandfather did not believe that my uncle was his son.

No Escape

But even in Baton Rouge, the truth lurked in the shadows. My grandfather's infidelity haunted me, a legacy of betrayal. There was never a real escape; even those weekends felt temporary, like a band-aid on deep, festering wounds.

Looking back, the lies and cover-ups suffocate me. I stand at the edge of understanding, but the journey to uncover the truth is just beginning.

Chapter 2

THE BETRAYAL

We lived in a tight knit community, literally all of my aunts lived across the court, but with different driveways. My grandmother and I would frequently go on walks in the projects to visit them. Sometimes I wasn't allowed to even go inside their homes. My family didn't like me, that was my grandmother's words. Was it because of this *secret* in our family? I was disowned by many of them and they were very cruel to me. They would say the most horrible things to me and about me. Funny thing is, I took it all in even though it made me feel worthless.

I can remember the times I was allowed to go to my auntie # 2's house. I was eleven years old by now. Two of my cousins were 15 going on 16 years old. I won't call it sexual assault since they seem to have amnesia. But, those cousins would always climb in the bed with me and literally force themselves inside of me. Did I know that it was ok? I knew that in my heart it was wrong, I was eleven years old. I always cried to go to my aunt's house because I grew up alone at my grandparent's house. I was lonely and wanted company. Even though I was being sexually abused, I just wanted to feel loved and accepted by my family in any way that I could. Later, when I revealed this secret about the sexual abuse, I was told that it was my fault. I was told that it was because I wore little dresses and didn't close my legs that my cousins raped me. Yep, everything was my fault, even though I was a little girl!

Being treated like an outsider would start to take its toll on me. While I was being raped at two of my aunt's houses, I would go to another aunt's house and she would tell me so many bad things about my mom. She would tell me the different lies that were told to me by my grandmother. That my mom was drugged, and that she was raped by a gang of boys, and was messing with married men.

There were a lot of things they would tell me as a child, I assume to confuse me and cover up the truth. I started normalizing this dysfunction. I never saw a way out; I just felt very different in my family. They never knew how to talk to me, they said that I would never be anything. They would call me bald headed and all kinds of curse words. It was very degrading, I then started saying, "I guess this *is* who I am"; I told myself.

After the card game there were no more birthdays and Christmas'. I didn't look forward to anything as a kid anymore. It's like they snatched that from me. So, when the kids would play for Christmas, all I wanted was this woman that I was going to see to tell me the truth. I had questions, why are you here, and how could you just leave me with so many answers?

It got lonely around the holidays. Kids would line up around asking for toys. I would sit alone at the Christmas tree, praying that my mom would walk through the door. I had some very dark nights and lonely days. With no love, and no communication; pretty much raising myself.

School was my escape, I found peace by being able to be around other people. My grandparents were illiterate, they couldn't read or write. They couldn't help me with my homework, so I got to see things differently at school.

I wore nice things, my grandparents gave me the material things. I think it was their way of saying that they "cared.' Deep down, I was broken and afraid. I was covering everything up like a mask.

My grandfather wasn't with the whole "chilling at other people's houses" thing. To him, that was a straight-up no-go. So, catching up with my friends outside of school or on weekends? Yeah, that wasn't happening. While everyone else was out having fun, I was locked down at home, like weekends and freedom weren't meant for me. I was forced to be around older family members on weekends and holidays. My grandparents always visited their siblings and other older family members; my life was a mess!

I felt like he was trying to keep me close to him, so that people would not find out the truth. All I had were my aunts' houses to go to, the isolation was real. I got treated differently than their children. I just felt like if their kids got into trouble, I got the backlash, for anything that happened. So out of all of my aunts, I would like to go to auntie #3's house.

Auntie # 3 had a daughter. Me and her were a couple of months apart. So, we grew up like sisters. I was always excited to go to her house until her oldest son started violating me. Whenever I would go there, he would actually take my clothes off, get in the bed when everybody went to sleep and do things to me that I was very uncomfortable with. I always wanted to go to that aunt's house, to play with my cousin. I overlooked the fact that my cousin would sexually abuse me every chance that he got. As I said before, it was just the price that I had to pay to not feel lonely and to have someone to play with. The fact that auntie # 3 said that I got what I deserved, wow I was only 11!

So, I stored all that away as a little girl and still tried to find happiness and peace beyond my family.

Deedee and I were about 7 years apart. Sometimes we would live in the same house whenever I stayed with auntie #2. I always wanted to go out with her and her best friend Moochie. They would comb my hair and I would sit back and watch them go to school dances. She was such a beautiful soul; I lived vicariously through her.

Once I became a teenager she became a bigger part of my life. She sent me to the OBGYN doctor when I got pregnant with my first child. In 1991 my aunts or grandmother would never teach me these things. She taught me how to be a young woman and got closer as I got older. She got married and her husband was tragically murdered. We stuck together.

My aunt, her mother would always try to put her out and put her hands on her. I would stand up for her, and they would put both of us out. When I became pregnant, they treated me like an adult and I would leave with her. She showed me the ropes and told me when I left, to never look back.

The Phone Call That Changed Everything

One day in 1988 my grandmother received a phone call. It was from the hospital concerning my grandfather. She told me that we were going to visit my grandfather, and it felt like any other visit. Once we got there, my grandfather was like his usual self, then, my grandmother made him mad.

I sat next to my grandfather, he held my hand and said that he was sorry. I was a bit confused about why he was apologizing. Yet, in my heart I knew. I loved this man, despite the pain he caused me and my mother

My grandmother then came over, and for whatever reason he didn't want to eat, so he started arguing with her. " No, I don't want it, I don't want no damn jello!" I heard my grandfather yelling.

They went back and forth for a while, so my grandmother decided to call for the nurse. By then a doctor and nurse had stepped into the room and we were asked to leave.

My grandfather was still screaming at the top of his lungs, then silence. My grandfather died right then and there. Crazy, I was left confused without any answers.

On his death certificate it read that he died of "anger."

Chapter 3

WHOA BABY! MY MAMA'S SURPRISE BABY AND THE BIRTH OF MY BABIES

After my grandfather passed, in 1988 I was 13, and that's when things started to change—especially me. I began rebelling, not just against my grandmother but against my whole family, especially my mom's siblings. My grandmother wasn't having any of that "sleeping over at friends' houses" or "going to school dances" stuff. She wasn't about that life, so I had to get creative.

Lucky for me, she had one weakness: bingo. Bingo started at 8 o'clock, she'd head out to play, and I knew I had until 11 to sneak out, run around with my homegirls, and get back before she stepped off that bingo bus. I had it down to a science, and I was living for those few hours of freedom. It felt like I was finally doing something for myself, at age 15. No rules and no restrictions. I was having the time of my life, even if I was cutting it close every time.

But my grandmother, she wasn't the same after my grandfather passed. She found her voice, and let me tell you, that voice was tough. It was like all that time she spent quietly when my grandfather was alive, she was just holding back. Now that he was gone, it all came pouring out, and she didn't hold back, especially with me. She went from being the sweetest lady you'd ever meet to this strict, angry version of herself. I swear, it was like living with her alter ego. I loved her, but at the same time, I was scared of this new person she'd become. It made me want to break free even more.

I didn't want to be in the same house with her at this point or around anyone in my family. So, when I got to middle school, I started hanging with a couple of girls and they had boyfriends.

Real Love?

Nobody in my family talked to me about boys, but I did experience sex 'cause I was violated at the age of 11, by my two cousins. I didn't think boys were attracted to me at the time. I didn't even think I was attractive at the time, I didn't think I was a pretty girl. So, one day my friend asked me to come around the avenue. It was like little sets in our hood, and that's what we called it.

I can remember that it was around Mardi Gras time in New Orleans and they had a parade passing on St. Charles. My friend was dating an older guy and his friend liked me. I didn't know why he liked me, 'cause I never felt attractive. I also at that time didn't have a desire for boys, he was much older than me. I was 15 and he was 19.

He showed me something that I guess I was looking for. He protected me. I had never felt protected before. There were so many times that I needed that protection, and that guidance. I didn't realize how much I was yearning for it. So when I found it, I didn't want to let it go.

The very first time we had sex; I got pregnant. I started to feel sick. I knew something was wrong with me. I told my grandmother that I wasn't feeling well. She just kept saying, "you keep running out of this house, no telling what you doing." She saw me always sneaking by his house 'cause she followed me one time. She told him she was gonna put him in jail. Actually, she put him in jail too. Right before I had my son. I had no idea why my body was going through changes.

My favorite cousin Deedee, told me that I needed to go to an OBGYN. Of course, I didn't know what that was. She already had a kid, so she sent me to her doctor, in which this doctor became like a father to me. He was located off Louisiana Ave.

During my first visit with him, he asked me if I knew anything about STDs. I told him I knew nothing. He then proceeded to educate me on the cause and effects of STDs, how many months I was, my due date, and answered all of my questions. I thank GOD for this man. He had so much patience with me and guided me along the way. He didn't even much want to see me 'cause I was young, but he did. He walked me through the whole process of my pregnancy. I eventually went into labor, and my grandmother said that I deserved to have a natural birth so that I could feel what *real* pain feels like.

Life or death

One day, my grandmother's cousin rolled in from Baton Rouge to visit us, and it happened to be Father's Day weekend. I ended up in the bathroom for what felt like an eternity, clutching my stomach and crying. It felt like a storm was brewing inside me, and I thought I just had to make a bowel movement. My body was going through these wild convulsions, and I had no idea what was happening. I screamed at the top of my lungs, desperate for someone to hear me.

That's when my grandmother's cousin yelled out, "Trina might be going into labor! You need to help her!" She dialed 911 and got me into an ambulance. Looking back, I can't help but wonder what would have happened if she hadn't been there. My grandmother? She had her own twisted views on pain and suffering. She believed

I needed to *learn a lesson,* and I wouldn't put it past her to let me stay in that bathroom, writhing in agony, thinking it was for my *own good.*

At that moment, it felt like God had orchestrated everything perfectly, waiting for that exact day for me to go into labor. He knew her cousin would be there to pull me back from the edge, to make sure I didn't get lost in that pain.

So, I went in the ambulance. Neither one of them showed up at the hospital. I found out that my baby was breech. My son was coming feet first and my pressure was going up. I didn't know anything about pressure. All the doctor kept saying was "code blue," and that he needed someone to sign some paperwork so that I could have an emergency c-section.

My pressure was going up, and my heart rate was dropping. The doctor needed to make a decision. He needed somebody to consent because I was still a minor.

Nobody showed up to give the doctor consent. He went with his instinct. He didn't care if he lost his license, he was losing me at that point! He had to cut and clip both sides of my uterus, then scrap some straps around my stomach and stretch my uterus to turn my son around to pull him out. I wound up having to get stitches and stayed in the hospital for about three days until my pressure went down. By this time, my son's father was incarcerated.

At this point I had just entered womanhood. Nothing about my life would ever be the same. Nobody ever told me that once you become a mother, especially a teenage mother; you better hold on for dear life because everything speeds up from here!

My son's father

My son's father was the ultimate hustler, always grinding and doing whatever it took to make ends meet. He came from a big family— ten siblings in total—and lost his mom at a young age. With so many mouths to feed, he felt the weight of the world on his shoulders and dropped out of school to take care of his family. He was my rock, my best friend, and I felt like we were building a future together. So, when he got locked up, it crushed me. I envisioned a life where we'd raise our son together, but instead, he was handed a 20-year sentence. He didn't come home until my son was 30. Thankfully, I kept my son close to his family; his sisters stepped up big time, helping me raise him in those crucial early years.

Just after giving birth, I found myself staring down three months in jail. My grandmother had finally had enough and filed charges against me for running away—this was the third time she called the cops on me. Standing before the judge in July of 1991 felt surreal. She was furious to see me again, and with my son's father just released before he got locked up again, he was subpoenaed to show up as well. My grandmother and my auntie #2 were there, pushing for the harshest penalties. My aunt was relentless, saying things like, "You need to do something with her! She had a baby for a grown man! Lock her ass up!" What else could I expect for her to say, when she treated her own kids so horribly.

When the judge started asking questions about why I'd been missing school, I answered honestly, saying I'd just had a baby and was going to finish school. But I was young and rebellious; when she demanded certain things from me, I shot back, "I'm not gonna do it." That didn't sit well with her at all. "If you're not going to comply, I'm sentencing you to three months in jail!" I couldn't believe it. "But I have a newborn!" I pleaded. "That's why I subpoenaed his dad," she replied coldly. "He'll raise him while you do your time."

I remember that day so clearly. My son's father, desperate and confused, asked the judge, "Can I do the three months? I don't know the first thing about raising a child. She needs to be with our son!" But she was firm: "No, she's going to jail!" Without a doubt my aunt and grandmother showed no mercy.

Locked up

They sent me to the Youth Study Center in New Orleans, and it was a brutal transition, being yanked away from my newborn. The place was chaotic; I ended up in a four-girl cell, with girls from all different wards . In New Orleans, there were beefs everywhere— uptown against downtown, and the lines were drawn deep. I got into a big fight, and they moved me to isolation—just me in a one-man cell for the next 90 days. I could only go to school and take a shower at night. I wasn't even allowed to call home or check on my son.

But then there was a guard named Elli who took pity on me. My cousin had called to get a message to me about my son being in ICU. He had caught pneumonia, and his food was backing up into his lungs. The doctors didn't know if he was going to make it. And still, my grandmother was relentless, pressing charges against my son's father for neglecting him. The judge sided with her and granted her custody. Now here I was dealing with doing 3 months in jail away from my son, my son nearly dying, and then being granted custody to the one lady who is the main cause of all of my trauma. My grandmother! It felt like such a slap in the face. I was raging inside but there was nothing that I could do. I was stuck, doomed to serve out the remainder of my sentence.

By the time I was released, I was 16, almost 17, and had to fight to regain custody of my son. In Louisiana, turning 17 with a kid meant you were considered an adult, which opened some doors.

I applied for low-income housing, hoping for a fresh start, but while I waited for my own place, I had to move back in with my grandma. It was supposed to be temporary—a stepping stone to something better. But then I met this guy at 1108, a teen club on Canal Street where we all used to hang. He was everything you'd expect to catch your eye—tall, slim, with gold teeth, pulling up in a ride that screamed money. They called him Tdub, and he was from Calliope, same as me. Funny how we'd never crossed paths before.

We started spending time together, and soon enough, I was pregnant. It would've been my second child, but I was still just a kid myself, living under my grandmother's roof. She wasn't going for that. I was terrified, so deep in love that I reached out to Tdub, telling him, "I'm pregnant, but we can't keep this baby." He didn't miss a beat. "I agree," he said, with no hesitation.

I had no idea where to start, so I called my OB, hoping for answers. He asked, "Are you sure this is what you want?" But how could I be sure when I barely knew what I was doing? I just knew I was scared, confused, and alone. Tdub, true to his word, sold his chain and took me to the abortion clinic. My mind told me it was right, but my heart? That was a different story. I buried that hurt, hoping it would fade.

Two years passed, and life was moving forward. I finally got a job as a cashier at Winn-Dixie, In New Orleans East. Finally, my name came up on the waitlist for housing. Here was my chance to create something different for me and my son. I was stepping out, determined to make a life that wasn't shadowed by everything I'd been through.

But at 19, I found out I was pregnant again—this time with my daughter. Her father and I had been on and off, and he was always in and out of jail. While I worked, I'd party with friends who became family. I was the life of the party, hitting every club, dancing and laughing until dawn. No drinks, no drugs—just dancing and wild nights that let me forget the pain, if only for a while.

But when it came to my kids, I was careful. I kept the chaos at a distance, determined that they wouldn't grow up feeling the weight of my past. It felt like I was breaking out piece by piece, moving forward one hard-earned step at a time.

Then, came the shock of a lifetime: I discovered my mother was pregnant too. The call came from the school where she was being held; they said she was expecting and was planning on having an abortion. I couldn't believe it. How was this even possible? She was supposed to be under the care of a facility for people with special needs. When I pressed for details about the pregnancy, they couldn't provide any answers. I was furious. Without a second thought, I told them not to proceed with the abortion.

The surprise baby

A few months later, I received another call—my mother was in the hospital giving birth to my brother in December 1994. I arrived at the hospital, still angry and confused. What could I expect? The whole situation felt like the biggest cover-up ever, and nobody had any answers. My mother was so out of it, heavily medicated, that she didn't even know what was going on. I held her hand and reassured her that everything would be okay. After the birth, they asked if I could take the baby, but I was struggling to keep my own kids alive. I was 18 years old with 2 kids. My grandmother and my mom's sisters all said no, so thankfully my mom's first cousin stepped in to take him. I was relieved, but he was born with some mental challenges due to all the medications they had my mom on.

To this day, I'm still searching for answers about how this pregnancy could have even happened. It felt like they were trying to cover up the truth. I can't imagine what my mom felt—being taken advantage of without her consent, having another child with a man who had violated her. It broke my heart to think about it. Crazy how her siblings surrounded her bed side again acting like this was her fault, putting the pressure on me trying to convince me that I should be responsible, crazy I know right! We decided to do a DNA test to confirm our suspicions about the secret that had been plaguing me for so long, was my mom also my sister?

With the help of two RN friends, we all got swabbed—my mom, my brother, and me. This was my chance to finally uncover the truth about my identity. When the results came back, I was stunned. The test showed that my mother and I were sisters and we share the same father. My grandfather is really my dad . My mother was actually my sister.

Now that she knows everyone who hurt her is gone, she's more open about her past. She tells me everything and then asks, "Are you okay?" I always reassure her that she's safe. I feel like my healing journey played a significant role in her recovery as well. My brother needs me too. I was absent from his life for so long, even though he would call me, telling me he loved me. I was always invited to his birthday parties, and while I made it to a few, I often made promises I couldn't keep. I struggled to cope with everything, and it was overwhelming.

The family had placed a burden on me, painting me as the bad child while I was just the victim. They said things like, "You're the bad one; your mama should've given you away. Why are they raising you?" It felt like they were trying to break me, and I was so upset. I wanted to sue the facility where my mother was, to hold them accountable, but my hands were tied. My grandmother still had control over everything, and I knew that one day the truth would come to the light.

The reality of motherhood

During this time, in 1993 I met a girl named Cookie. We formed a close bond. I was pregnant with my first daughter and we were both living in the same apartments in the East. Remember the ones I mentioned with my first apartment? Yep, that one. I remember it like it was yesterday, I was giving my son a birthday party. He was turning two at the time and she came over and introduced herself. As time passed we became close like sisters, full of ups and downs. Whenever she dated someone, I would end up dating his best friend. We were inseparable, partying together and often getting into fights. I had two kids at this point, and she had one. I was still trying to figure out life, even though I was living on my own. My grandmother stayed in my life. When I tell you it was nothing she would not do for me or my kids. But it had to come with rules. The minute I wouldn't allow her to run my life she would take everything back from me, this became normal to me.

She couldn't live her life unless I was a part of it and she would show up at my apartment in rage and anger, putting my friends out and going as far as to tell guys me and my friends were hoes. This was where the anger and hate started to build up between me and my grandmother. I didn't understand where the anger came from. In 1996, around the age of 21, I found out I was pregnant with my third child. At his time I was living on the westbank, and had lost my housing in the East.

Later, I learned my son's father was in a serious relationship and his family wanted nothing to do with my child. As always, I didn't pursue child support from any of my kids' fathers. I worked hard and did things I was not proud of to provide for them, even while living off assistance. I tried hard to provide a safe space for my children and attended family functions, even though I often felt uncomfortable. I accepted the pain and trauma my family caused me just to be around them. I visited my grandmother occasionally,with my kids she played a major role. Even with the trauma that she caused, I still wanted my kids to have a relationship with her. I loved her past all the lies.

Also at this time, my mom wouldn't talk to me or accept visits. My kids up to this point had no idea that my mom even existed. I hid her away and told them that she had died; afraid to open up the Pandora's box of pain that it would cause them to know the truth about my family. So, I stopped visiting my mother. I thought I was hurting her, and to be honest it was hurting me; so I stayed away.

My family had their moments of fun, and I didn't know any better than to normalize the dysfunction. I always showed up for every family event, believing everything was okay, never saying anything bad about them to my children. In fact, like I mentioned before, my children didn't even know about my mother until I was 35 years old. During this time, I was seeing a psychiatrist because my family was trying to build a case against me, claiming I was hallucinating. I was overwhelmed, but I enrolled in a program that helped pay my rent as long as I saw a counselor.

Once, I had to move back in with my grandmother with my kids, but that was short-lived. My mother's brother was still alive and battling addiction. One Christmas, he stole all my children's gifts. In a fit of rage, I threw chicken grease on him, which led my grandmother to arrest me for it. She sided with her son over me and kicked me and my kids out. It was storming that night, and thankfully a friend—who I called my cousin—came to pick us up and let us stay with her for a while.

I lived with them for about five months, but there was a catch: I had to date her boyfriend's partner to stay there. I was essentially being forced into a relationship with someone I didn't like just to put a roof over my kids' heads. At that point, sex didn't hold much meaning for me anymore, especially after being violated as a child. It felt like an easy way to cope, so I went along with it. I refused to stay with any of my aunts, and thankfully, I never had to.

Chapter 4

I CREATED MY OWN FAMILY;
THE CHAOS CONTINUES

Life hit different with my third child. He was different. While my firstborns were the norm, my youngest? He was colorful. I'd catch him in my daughter's clothes, strutting around like he owned the place, playing with hair like he was on the set of a fashion show. But the streets weren't ready for that. Back then, the LGBTQ+ scene wasn't what it is today. The whispers and sneers behind my back were relentless, calling my baby all kinds of names. It cut deep. My family? They didn't know how to deal either. They just couldn't see beyond their narrow lens. I knew he was different, but I also knew there was nothing wrong with that. Love, after all, isn't bound by gender.

The marriage from hell

Not long after, at about age 22, I found myself tied to a younger man. A slick dude from the West Bank who was raising his siblings while making a name for himself in the drug game. Our marriage was a whirlwind, a courthouse affair on the other side of the river. But life threw me a curveball. A lawsuit came my way, the cops kicked in my door without a warrant, we made the news, and I was now in the money. Raking in a quick $10,000 from the apartment complex for allowing this to happen. At that point, it felt like a blessing from God.

We hit the bank on Canal Street, cashing that check and stuffing the cash into a duffle bag like it was some prize we'd won. But money can't fix everything. My husband was drowning in a bottle while I hustled at work. Before I knew it, we spiraled into a storm of domestic violence. He broke my arm, and in a moment of pure desperation, I stabbed him back. That made headlines too. Within the first 30 days of our marriage, we were both arrested. I got off, but he had to serve 30 days in the pen.

I wanted out. I was ready to annul the whole thing, but no judge was having it. They insisted on pre-counseling first. When he got out, he bounced back to Mississippi without a second thought, and I didn't chase him. I didn't feel the need to fight for a divorce, so we remained tied together in marriage until 2016.

Moving to Kenner was my next step, away from the chaos of New Orleans. I settled in low-income housing and began to build a new life, meeting people from all walks. My kids were a force, often clashing like storm clouds. My son endured hell because of his identity. In a world where acceptance was scarce, I became his shield, navigating a path to protect him from the harsh realities outside. I put him on private buses, anything to keep him safe. My daughter took on the role of defender, always ready to throw down for her brother.

Then there was my oldest son, who fell in line with his dad's crew. I kept him close to that side of the family, hoping to shield him from the streets that threatened to swallow him whole. But life was a mess. I was grappling with homelessness, family betrayal, and nights spent with men just to keep a roof over my kids' heads. It was a wild ride, and through it all, I fought tooth and nail to keep my family together.

Building my own family

Let me tell you, the streets don't owe me nothing! In New Orleans, I ran through every club and corner. My name rang out, loud and clear. I rolled with a crew of girls who became my sisters, creating a bond forged in fire. With all the family dysfunction, I built my own family—stronger, tighter, and more resilient.

I took my share of abuse from friends, drawn to the same pain I was carrying. Hurt people hurt people, and I was a magnet for trouble. My favorite cousin,Deedee, my rock, showed me the ropes. She was everything—a big sister, a mentor, a beacon of light. But the darkness crept in when she passed away at just 28. We were about 7 years apart, so I was still 21 at this time.

I always wondered why her mom treated her so poorly. Her house was next door, a constant reminder of the turmoil she faced. I stood up for her, defended her, but when they kicked her out, I had to leave too. The last time I saw her, she came to me with a heaviness in her heart, sharing her fears about an impending surgery. She was scared, and I was helpless, caught in the ignorance of youth.

In March of 2000, she left for work, and later called me, whispering something that would change my life forever. "You're pregnant," she said, and I laughed it off. But she urged me, "Whatever you do, don't go back to that family." Just hours later, the phone rang, bringing news I wasn't ready for. She had been rushed to the hospital. Her mother's indifference was palpable, but I couldn't ignore the gravity of the situation.

Why did she have to go so soon?

When I arrived at the hospital, it felt surreal. They led me to the chapel, and confusion clouded my mind. Why were we here? My aunt stood there, stone-faced, not shedding a tear. Meanwhile, my grandma crumpled to the floor, the weight of grief too much to bear. I pushed through to see my cousin one last time. She looked peaceful, hair styled, and makeup done like she knew her fate. The doctors did everything they could, but youth wasn't enough to save her. My auntie #2, her mother was bitter and cold. I couldn't believe it. My cousin was so young, so beautiful. She was like a sister to me and she was now gone.

Also, during this chaos, my cousin's brother—who had violated me—was locked up for murder, a dark twist in our already broken family tree. I didn't know how to feel; love and pain intertwined like a knot I couldn't untie. Yet, I still visited him, because that's what family does, right?

Then came my fourth child, September 30, 2000. A miracle little girl, born from the ashes of grief. The same baby that my cousin DeeDee told me I was pregnant with before she died. With DeeDee gone, I also felt a weight of responsibility to her kids, like I did my own. They fell into the care of a woman who didn't deserve them, her mom. I was thrust into the role of a mother of four, still navigating my own grief and trauma, and being there for DeeDee's kids as well. Life was a whirlwind and I found myself being swept up.

Years later, I had a visitation from my cousin DeeDee—draped in white beyond the grave, she said, "Check on my son." It was his birthday. I felt the urgency and reached out. He was living life on the edge, but that night, I also had a nightmare that he'd been shot. I couldn't shake the feeling, so I asked my son's father to check on him. The news was bad, but not fatal. He was alive, but the fight was just beginning. He had been fighting and was arrested. Family bailed him out that night, but then....

About a week or so later, I got the call no one wanted to hear, he'd been shot over 15 times. The drive to the scene was a blur—sirens, screams, and a thousand questions I couldn't even answer. My hands were shaking as I dialed his grandmother, Auntie #2. Your grandson's been shot," I said. Her response hit me harder than anything: "I'm not coming down there. They might kill me too." She said coldly.

I couldn't wrap my head around it. How could his own blood, his own grandmother, care more about her safety than her grandson's life? But me? I was his aunt, I felt like I didn't have the luxury of turning away.

When we got to the hospital, they rushed him straight into surgery. Chaos was everywhere—doctors shouting orders, family wailing, people praying. But I refused to let doubt creep in. "If he's got a heartbeat, we fight," I told the doctors. I was in their faces, making sure they knew we weren't giving up.

His grandmother showed up eventually, but her words just added salt to the wound. "He's gone die! Just pull the plug; he's gonna die anyway." Her voice was cold, resigned, like she'd already buried him in her mind.

But I wasn't having it. I looked those doctors dead in the eye and said, "Don't listen to her. If he has a heartbeat, you do everything you can. I don't care what she's saying." I wasn't letting anyone give up on him—not his family, not the doctors, not even him.

They asked who had custody of him, I said " she does, but I don't care." Luckily they didn't listen to my auntie. He lived, and he is 35 years old today. I went on to help him. HALLELUJAH! What a wonderful God we serve. If it were up to my auntie, his grandmother, he would be in a grave. It wasn't his time!

The doctor said that the only reason why he lived was because he was popping Percocets before the shooting. Meaning, he had a lot of pills in his system that kept his blood flowing. Without the pills he was popping, he would be dead.

After they did the surgery, he was in a coma, and in ICU. His stomach was bust wide open. He had no intestines. The doctor only gave him a few weeks to live. I said, the devil is a liar!

Back from the brink of death

Every hour you could go see him. I stayed there every hour and I prayed and I prayed. I held his hand and I just prayed. I was like, "I got this, he just can't die." My auntie was like, "I don't know why you up there, 'cause he just gone die." They were so negative. One day I got a phone call from the hospital and they said that it wasn't anymore that they could do for him. They were going to have to discharge him. I told him that I did not have a car. I also said that his grandmother isn't going to get him and asked if they could ambulance him to me. They did! I had moved back to Baton Rouge at that time and they sent him to me in an ambulance. A whole hour and forty minutes away. I had never seen that!

They gave him two weeks to live. He could talk, and he was having nightmares. He had a tube and his stomach was open. So when we fed him by mouth, it was just coming out of his stomach. Everything, just everything, you saw all of his guts.

All my children were there crying. They couldn't take it. I was working, and he had a little bell that I told him to ring. I quit my job and I said, " I'm gonna have to find some type of help." So I called every doctor, and every nurse. They told me that they didn't think that his body was strong enough to do the surgery, but this was the surgery that he needed to close his stomach up.

So, I started feeding him little Ensure drinks. He was getting a little appetite for things like noodles; but then it would just come outta his stomach. I didn't know what to do at this point. I was moving to Atlanta, and I was also sick at the time. I didn't know that I had the same thyroid cancer that his mama had. I was really getting weak. I didn't want to give up on him and I didn't want him to leave. I wound up finding some doctors that would do the surgery, but I didn't know if his body would be able to take it. He may die in the surgery. So, one day while I was talking to him. I asked him, "Do you wanna have this surgery?"

I then explained that if you lay here, you're gonna die anyway. "He then said, "I wanna have the surgery."

He was in surgery for about seven hours, but he lived and has one child. I moved him to Atlanta with me. He stayed in Atlanta 'til about last year. He's back in Louisiana now. That took me for a run for my money 'cause I helped raise him like my own son. I felt obligated not to walk away from him even though his own grandma said "let him die." That's my family for ya! Every twist in this story feels like a test, but I refuse to back down. Family is messy, but it's all I know, and I'll do anything to keep us together

But on the other hand, my family was praying for me to die. Sad to say but real.

The system failed my mother

I had a lot going on at this time. To say that life was life-ing is a pure understatement. It's hard to tell my mama's story without telling my own, you see; she was my driving force. From childhood, to motherhood, sicknesses, and failed marriages. My mother was the reason that I kept going. By this time my kids were fighting a lot, and I had a gay son. I still found time to go back to see my cousin's children. I felt like she was the only one who took up time with me. So I felt obligated not to leave her kids stuck out there. My auntie failed my cousin's children, his sister, my cousin's other child ended up doing time in prison. I helped her out too, as much as I could. I had met another dude and had another child at this time. Now I am around 27 years old and a mother of 5.

My fifth child came in Feb 2003 with a guy named Edward. He did time, and I ended up having a baby on him. I met Edward in 1998, he ended up going to jail for almost 2 years. He was released In 2000, the same day I went into labor with my daughter. What a coincidence! When he got out, I was so done with the whole baby-making scene, but since we had been in a long-term relationship, I felt like I owed him a kid. I was also feeling guilty by having a kid with another man while he was locked up. Because of all of the chaos in my life I was having baby after baby, and looking for love in all the wrong places. I don't know if it was to fill some kind of void, but I kept doing it. Now don't get me wrong, my daughter and all of my children are my biggest blessings, but it makes you wonder the *why* behind it all. Isn't it wild how being surrounded by dysfunction for so long can have you making some seriously messed-up choices? The thought of "owing" this man a child should scream insanity, but it doesn't. When you've been stripped of your worth, you end up feeling like you owe everyone else something—while your own desires go ignored. You'll chase after giving others the world while your own dreams collect dust.

At this time my life is slowing down, I'm a mother of 5 and I'm starting to have some undetermined health problems. I'm now trying to pull my life together, and start over in Kenner outside of New Orleans. Life was still an everyday battle, but just when I thought I was settling down..the biggest disaster of them all hits.

Hurricane Katrina

The system failed my mother, and it hit me like a ton of bricks. Over the years, they shoved her into a school for people with disabilities—despite her having none—and I can only guess at the dark secrets they swept under the rug. I visited her before Katrina, where they'd placed her in some independent living situation. I brought pictures of me and the kids, thinking it would brighten her space. Then the storm hit, and we were all evacuating. I tried to reach the woman running the independent living facility, but she ghosted me. Her phone went dead, just like my hopes.

I was frantic, scouring databases to see if they'd even bothered to fill out my mother's food stamp information. Nothing. When I finally tracked her down, I discovered they had been cashing in FEMA checks in her name, while she was left behind. Yes, they straight-up abandoned my mama during Hurricane Katrina! Once the chaos subsided, I turned to the news. Channel Two in Baton Rouge aired my story, detailing my mother's mild disabilities and how the company was supposed to care for her but left her to drown. With over 1,392 lives lost and $186 billion in damages, it was a national catastrophe. New Orleans has never truly bounced back from that.

That's when I got the call from folks in Mississippi. They saw me on the news. My mama was all the way out there, but they wouldn't let me come get her; they insisted she was *fine*. I got a picture confirmed, and they took her to the hospital for a check-up. Eventually, they moved her back to New Orleans once things cleared up. They threw her a birthday party that I attended, bringing the kids with me from Atlanta, and her sisters came too. When she walked away from the celebration, it was clear she just never vibed with that side of the family.

This wasn't my first rodeo with hurricanes or with life throwing punches. Another storm hit in 2012, and that was the last time I laid eyes on my mother. I had left, packed up, and moved to Atlanta in 2014 without a single goodbye to her or my brother. Just up and left. But, like always, my hands were tied—Grandma was still her next of kin, and she held all the power over what happened with my mother.

Looking back, it's no wonder I was getting sick. I was carrying too much, trying to carry the weight of this family while my body was breaking down. That's when I developed thyroid cancer—the same disease that took my cousin's life. Over fourteen years, full of anxiety, everything came racing at me all at once. I was left alone with my kids to die. I even faced breast cancer twice, convinced each day could be my last. I had no one to turn to but God.

Sick and outta my mind

I couldn't understand it, every time I went to the doctor, they would tell me that I was crazy, but I was deteriorating. I could not swallow at all. It felt like I would choke if I did. The doctor said that it was mental and treated me as if I was some kind of mental patient. Then I came across a nurse who said that she recognized my symptoms and ordered a scan of my lungs.

How we got here

I started having panic attacks at an early age. I believe that I swallowed a lot of the dysfunction in my life and it was now causing me problems with my throat. I also never felt like I had a voice, I kept everything inside and I feel like all of these emotions backed up and were causing the problems.

You know, I think panic attacks started creeping in when I was just a kid, but I didn't know it then. I swallowed down all that dysfunction, all that toxicity, watching my grandfather hurl insults at my grandmother. The way he treated her was nothing short of abusive. His eyes? Cold as ice. He looked like he was free from a single worry, no conscience at all. People ask if he ever touched me, and honestly? I can't say I have bad memories of him. He was always too busy drinking, too busy not being there, leaving me to fend for myself at home. However, I did hear that he touched other relatives, even raping the woman who is now raising my brother. Yep! You heard that right. Crazzzyyyyyy!

Then taking those trips to visit my mom in those facilities, I felt that anxiety creep in and knot my stomach. I was never nurtured the way a girl should be, and I sure as hell didn't get the counseling I needed. I held that pain in while I went to school, masking it all. Nobody knew what was going down behind closed doors. I hid it all with a smile. I threw myself into friendships, calling their families my own. I was embarrassed—my reality felt like a dark cloud hanging over me. So, I ran away from home, seeking refuge wherever I could find it, trying to escape a place that felt more like a prison than a home.

I was already violated at a young age, cousins taking what wasn't theirs. It messed with my self-esteem, made me feel like I had to give it up to keep a guy interested. Nobody taught me about self-worth. Growing up around all that trauma? I was drowning in anxiety, and I dragged it all into adulthood, thinking I could shake it off just because I was older now. I bought nice things, filled my life with new friends, and called their moms "Mom" like that would fill the void.

But I was wearing a mask, living a double life, suffering in silence with anxiety and depression. It hit me like a ton of bricks after Katrina. My childhood traumas came rushing back, haunting me for over 15 years. I dealt with anxiety and depression, but I also had to face two surgeries to remove my thyroid and a tumor growing inside my throat. For 14 years, I couldn't eat. It wasn't just the tumor; it was the anxiety and all the wear and tear I'd bottled up from my past—the trauma I buried deep inside. I've been through five kids with five different fathers, two marriages, and one relationship I regret deeply.

Yeah, I beat the cancer, but depression took my mind. I had to see a counselor who told me straight up: if I kept everything bottled in, I'd never heal. That's when I realized I had to let my story out to break free. It was either die with this silence or speak my truth. So, I chose me. I started sharing my story, journaling, and eventually made my way onto a t.v show to tell the world what happened. That's when my healing journey truly began. Believe it or not, I only started eating again three years ago, after fourteen years

So, let's break this down.

How does someone not eat for 14 years?

It's all in the mind, I swear. People think curses aren't real, but trust me, they are. It was like a dark cloud over me, weighing me down. I felt like the enemy was trying to take me out because if I stopped eating, I was a goner. He didn't want me to share my story, didn't want me to heal. I was drinking multiple Ensures per day to stay alive.

But God brought people into my life to lift me up, and now here I am, eating and telling my truth. This isn't just for me; it's for my mama's freedom too.

It was terrifying. At that point, I had five kids, and they were all young. My oldest was around 20, but the rest were still at home, and they watched me spiral. I stopped driving, stopped grocery shopping, stopped caring about anything. I felt like I was just lying there, waiting for death. My kids thought I'd drop dead any day. And then, three years ago, I went through a messy divorce. My second husband? Toxic doesn't even begin to cover it. He ended up arrested for sex trafficking young girls. My life was a total wreck!

I moved to Florida, and that's when those suicidal thoughts hit hard—my youngest son had just left for college. I was alone, really alone, and had to face myself in the silence. I told my son I was packing up for Florida, looking for peace. "I need to find myself," I said. He looked at me and said, "Mom, if you didn't find peace in Atlanta, you won't find it in Florida. You're just taking yourself with you." He was right, but I was determined to try. The same way that I moved to Atlanta in search of a better life.

Once arriving in Atlanta, we stayed in a hotel for 5 months, then after not being able to afford to stay there any longer, I moved in with a friend who let us live with her. Thank God for her! I would have to drive 1 ½ hours to drive them to school in the morning, sleep in the car all day until they got out, then drive back 1 ½ hours back home in the evenings, because that's all the gas that I had. I was exhausted and deteriorating daily. I eventually got a stable apartment for me and my kids.

One evening on the way home from going to get the kids I got short winded. I was rushed to the hospital causing my oldest daughter to come rushing down to Atlanta. It was a fall day, November of 2014. I remember it like yesterday. We sat in the emergency room waiting on test results to come back. The doctors came in and said everything looked fine. My daughter was not going for it. She said my mother is slowly losing weight and she won't eat. I was stressed out to the max. I was going through a divorce and my health was failing all at the same time. I thought that Florida would be my new escape.

I met my second husband on Facebook in 2013. He would like my pictures and hit me up in my dm. We got married in January of 2019. He spoiled me with a big house, nice clothes, cars, and everything that I wanted. However, he was a liar and a cheater. Also during this time I had my first surgery. What I learned was, the only person I could change was myself. I went through all kinds of hell with this man! I wore it well though, covering up all of the dysfunction with a smile but I was going down hill, and fast!

In my first abusive relationship, I felt like a deer in headlights— frozen and powerless. When I entered my second marriage, I was more aware of the warning signs, yet I still believed I could change him. Mentally I knew I wasn't ready for a relationship. He was ultimately arrested on two felony counts of trafficking a fifteen year old girl, who was a runaway, and everything really spiraled from there. We separated and eventually, my youngest son graduated and was now heading to Jackson State for his first year, ready to play for Dion Sanders.

After moving to Florida, I was still reaching out to my ex, trying to collect alimony. I had become accustomed to the life that he provided and I didn't want it to stop. But he ghosted me, and wouldn't take my calls. I went to have surgery and he moved back in with his ex. Yes, he left me at one of the roughest times of my life! We were still getting bills at my old place in Atlanta, and then I found out he opened a cell phone in his name for another woman he was with. I called the number, and the girl answered. "Yeah, I'm the girl he was seeing before you."

I couldn't believe it. I was like, "Are you serious?" I was ready to drag him to court. He was telling her, "Stop saying that; I'm already going to court." I couldn't help but laugh at the mess of it all. He was supposed to be paying me every week, but he was dodging it. He sent me some money—maybe twice—but at that point, I didn't even care. I was just being petty.

Little did I know, my son wouldn't get picked as a starter at Jackson State, and I ended up having to cough up almost $8,000 for his tuition. That was money I had stashed away to keep my life in Florida afloat.

So there I was, drowning in bills, rent stacking up, and feeling like rock bottom was my new permanent address. I was at the end of my rope, so low that I actually put my kids, my ride-or-die Carla, and my cousins Tamika and Keisha in a group chat. I texted them like, "By the time y'all read this, I might not even be here." Then I downed a dozen of my anxiety pills, thinking I'd just drift off and never have to face another problem.

Luckily, my daughter had been my rock through it all, helping me move to Florida because I was too messed up to drive myself. Panic attacks were eating me alive, but I needed my car with me, so she stepped up, saying, "I'll drive your stuff down; you just catch a plane." Then she got this feeling and called the apartment, begging them to break down the door. They stalled, talking about the law and procedures, but she wasn't playing. She told them, "I'll send you the texts. My mom needs help." When they finally showed up, I woke up in an ambulance. And that's when I found out my so-called best friend—who I'd called my sister—had called asking, "Did she die?" She didn't ask if I was okay or if I needed anything. That was my wake-up call.

After that, my husband was supposed to come down to sign some papers, but my kids were like, "He better not show his face here." They were ready to stand up and protect me. Then the doctor came in, asking if I was really suicidal, and I just told him, "Nah, I just wanted to sleep and not wake up."

Eventually, I reconnected with my friend Natasha and Carla, my true lifelines. They were there emotionally and financially.

Natasha surprised me with a birthday party—the first one I'd had in forever. She kept it real about her own struggles, and I finally felt like I could breathe, like I didn't have to keep pretending I was fine. I opened up, told her about the eviction notice, and she didn't even flinch. She said, "I got you," and rallied some of my friends. They chipped in and came up with the money to keep me housed.

Meanwhile, Carla was there with that real talk, saying, "Come back home to Atlanta. You own a house here." That was the push I needed. I packed up, facing those panic attacks head-on, and drove back to Atlanta, feeling like I was finally reclaiming my life. And let me tell you, we all need a friend like Carla.

Things slowly started turning around. I got a receptionist job at Hyundai, trying to rebuild, one day at a time. My daughter nudged me to call my grandma, saying she'd been worried sick. I didn't want to, but after some prayer, I picked up the phone. Hearing her voice brought a peace I hadn't felt in ages. She told me, "Forget that man. You're strong. You'll find someone better." She even offered to co-sign for a new car since mine was barely hanging on.

It felt like a fresh start, a new chapter where I could finally take control of my life again. I was stepping back into the world with a sense of hope and the knowledge that, no matter what, I had real support behind me.

Chapter 5

THE END OF AN ERA

$\mathcal{M}$y cousin carried the insurance on my grandmother. She told Grandma she had to drop it because her business tanked after the pandemic. That policy was a chunk of change because of Grandma's age, and I had no clue they were even beefing about it.

One day, my baby daughter was chilling at Grandma's place and called me in a panic. Grandma was yelling, "What am I gonna do if I die?" She was 94 but still moving around like she owned the place. She was stressed, talking about needing to borrow money for her own burial, and I was at work just trying to hold it together.

I told my daughter, "I already picked out a car; I just need a co-signer." That morning, while I was at work, Grandma had already called the finance manager herself! Now, let me tell you, my grandma couldn't read or write, but she knew how to handle that phone and give out her info like a boss.

By the time I got to the dealership, they had the car parked right in front, ready to roll. The finance manager pulled me aside, saying, "Your grandma called. It's a go!" I was like, "What? No way!" But it was true. This car was nice—fully loaded and everything. I was used to luxury by now with my kids from my husband, but a Hyundai? I had no idea what I was missing until now. I was just grateful to God for it.

I called Grandma to thank her, and she was like, "No problem." I felt like everything was falling into place for a reason, like God knew I'd need wheels soon.

Then my cousin Meke hit me up, talking about her sister's 50th birthday party, saying, "Yo, you gotta come through." I was like, "Say less. I'm in. Just pick up my Grandma, and don't tell her I'm coming."

Now, Grandma's a trip—she doesn't play about her time. When I called her up to check in, she was already giving me the rundown: "Meke was supposed to pick me up hours ago, and I've been ready!" Meanwhile, I was halfway to the party, just listening and smiling, knowing she had no idea I was on my way.

I hit Meke up as soon as I got to the spot. "I'm coming through the door now," I told her, and she was all set for the surprise. The second I stepped in, it was like the whole room shifted. When Grandma turned and saw me, her face lit up, and I swear it was like I'd just given her the world. It was one of those moments that made every struggle and every challenge all worth it.

Our last days together

Man, that last picture I got with my grandma is everything. It hits differently, you know? We were taking so many photos, and she was smiling like she hadn't in a long time. But what stuck with me was how tight she hugged me. Now, my grandma? She wasn't the type to say "I love you" or even hug like that, but for those few days; she couldn't stop. She kept hugging me, kissing me, and I just kept snapping pictures, like, "You are a beautiful woman." My grandma was gorgeous, no lie.

Her sister even said, "Girl, you are the light of my sister's eyes." It felt so real. That night, we even shared a bed at my aunt's house—like old times. I had to wake her up the next morning. I was about to hit the Saints game, and it took me about five minutes to shake her awake. When she finally woke up, she looked off, like her memory was slipping or something. She sat up, looked at me, and said, "I'm tired, Trina." I'm like, "Tired of what, Grandma?"

She just raised her hand and said, "I'm ready to go. It's God's time." I froze. I'm like, "Ready to go where?" She said, "I'm just tired, baby." So I held her hands and started praying for her. Then she got up, her whole energy switched, and she called my aunt in the room. She was going off, cussing everyone out like, "I'm sick of y'all. Y'all act like I owe you something, but I'm done. I only owe Trina and my baby daughter an apology."

She looked at me and said, "Trina, I'm not mad you told your story. You got more courage than me, and I couldn't fight your grandfather. I want you to talk, write that book. I don't care what anyone says—I'm about to go, I'm so sorry my baby, I'm so sorry. " I didn't even realize what she was saying because she was still talking about spending Thanksgiving at my house the next week. However, she apologized. The apology that I had been longing to hear. She finally felt sorry for all of the damage and all of the pain. I still couldn't help but wonder, is it too late? I didn't know how to feel. Should I be mad, angry, or should I feel sorry for her? Was she a victim too or a victimizer? My head was spinning, but I wanted to hear her out. I decided to leave it alone for another time, however that time would never come.

Our final days

We had this crazy day at the Saints vs. Falcons game in New Orleans—my son, his dad, my grandma, and aunt, all together. My grandma shocked me when she said that she wanted to go, it wasn't like her. The game was lit, and I swear, Grandma was lighting up the whole stadium with her energy. She was all smiles, and my son was like, "Why you gotta take a picture?" I looked at him and said, "Because this might be the last one with her." He thought I was crazy, but something in me just knew.

About a week later, November 16th, it was my daughter's birthday. I was in Atlanta when I got a call from my brother. He said Grandma wasn't waking up. My brother/uncle was losing it, thinking it was his fault because he'd given her cold medicine the night before. He was already battling mental health issues, and now he's thinking he caused her stroke. I jumped in my car and headed straight down, no hesitation.

That was the day everything changed.

My grandma had called me earlier, but I missed it—two missed calls at 3 a.m. My heart sank because my brother had been trying to wake her up all morning, and she wasn't responding. They rushed her to the hospital, but I knew... deep down, I knew. It was her time.

Her connection with my kids was special, especially my daughter, who was struggling to handle it all. They were close, and Grandma co-signed on her apartment. When she had the stroke, it happened on my daughter's birthday, and it hit her hard—like a part of her was gone too. My daughter couldn't even bring herself to visit Grandma in the hospital after that. It was like everything came full circle, you know? Grandma gave us all she could, and in the end, she was just tired. But she left her mark, no doubt about it.

Man, it was wild. We were at the hospital, and they came out telling us, "*Ain't no coming back from that stroke.* Both sides of her brain were filled with blood," they said. So the doctors started asking us if she ever told us what to do? And I already knew. She told me straight up, "*If something happens to me, don't revive me.*" She wasn't about to be in a nursing home or laid up like that, and I respected it. Me and her sister knew it.

But my other aunt/sister? Nah, she was acting differently. Guilt was eating her up 'cause she never treated her mama right. So now, here we are, the doctors saying it's time to let go, but she's talking 'bout *revive her.* I'm thinking, *What's there to revive? She doesn't want that. She's weak, and the doctors even said it's not any coming back from this stroke.* But sister/auntie # 2 acting like she has something to prove, like she's tryna make up for all the time she treated her badly. Trying to drag it out, and keep her suffering.

They ended up doing what they wanted. Put her in a nursing home—something my grandma would've hated. I wasn't trying to leave New Orleans, but back to Atlanta I went. When I touched down, I got this call from my son's dad. He had just come from a Saints game down in Florida. Dude sounded sick, coughing badly. I told him, "*That cold doesn't sound right, you need to get it checked out.*" He promised if he didn't feel better by morning, he'd go to the hospital.

It's so hard to say goodbye...

Later that night, I woke up like something heavy hit my chest. My anxiety flared up crazy, so I took my meds. Next thing I know, I'm getting a Facebook call—his cousin calling me at 3 AM. Who does that? As soon as I saw the name pop up, I knew. I didn't even pick up the phone yet and I just knew. I answered and he said, *"That boy gone."* It felt like the world crashed in on me.

I start banging on my son's door, screaming. He's confused, asking me what's going on, and I had to tell him. I hated it, breaking my son's heart like that. He punched a hole in the wall. *"I've been calling him all day, Mom,* he said. *He never missed Christmas—he always sent money."* They found the envelope in his car, cash ready for our son. That man was dying, and he still had my boy on his mind.

I had to go back to New Orleans again, 'cause Edward didn't have any family left. But the cousin he was living with. His mom and dad had gone, his brother too. It was just me and his kids. And get this—right before he passed, he had told the kids he had a baby with some girl. Turns out it was true, a kid with some young girl we grew up with. Creeped me out. Like, if I'd known, I'd have choked him back to life just to ask him what the hell he was thinking!

His oldest daughter gave me the honor to help with the service. I picked out his clothes, and made sure that he looked right. Even after all that, I couldn't shake the feeling though—my grandma fighting for her life, me holding on to my mother, and now Edward was gone too. Life was just pulling me in every direction, and I didn't know how to keep going. But I had to...

They all trusted me to handle things and to keep it together. I just wish he'd taken care of himself; even though he'd outlived what the doctors predicted, that man wasn't done. I wasn't ready for him to go. RIP Edward, always in my heart.

I was there, standing front and center, watching it all unfold. He passed away on December 21st, but they held his body until January 14th for the funeral. That's a long time to wait, a long time to sit with the loss. It was surreal. I had just been fussing at him a few weeks before because our son needed a car for school. He told me not to worry, and promised he'd take care of it. Turns out, the car he was talking about ended up being his—just like that, it became our son's when he passed. It's wild how life plays you sometimes.

What I didn't know back then was that he had already made his peace. He was sick, and he knew it. He went around, making his rounds, saying quiet goodbyes, but he kept it to himself, and carried it alone. Edward had high blood pressure his whole life and never wanted to take his meds—living like it couldn't catch up to him. The first heart attack hit him when he was staying with me in Atlanta. I dragged him to the hospital, and the doctors said his blood pressure was so high it was shutting down his kidneys. His organs were fighting just to keep up, but he still wouldn't listen.

I'll never forget that one night he called me from New Orleans, talking about how he'd been sitting on the toilet too long. I knew something was wrong. I told him, "You better call 911 right now." He didn't want to, but finally, he did. And when I called back, the ambulance picked up, saying they were rushing him to the hospital. I called my daughters, told them, "Y'all better get over there and check on him." They showed up, and there he was, FaceTiming me, and cracking jokes with my girls. He always had that smile, like he wasn't gonna let us see him sweat. But deep down, he knew.

He made this Facebook post one day, saying how the doctors only gave him a year to live, but he made it to see his son go to college. He pushed through three more years on sheer willpower alone, but in the end, it was too late. He'd finally started taking his meds, but surgery wasn't even an option anymore.

The last time I saw him, it was like seeing a ghost. He showed up to our son's football game, and I almost didn't recognize him. He was so small, so different from the Edward I'd known. I greeted him with, "How you doing, sir?" and he just looked at me and said, "Trina." It hit me right then. He sat by the fence, just watching our son play, all quiet and distant, like he was carrying a world of secrets. After the game, he disappeared into the shadows before I could ask him anything.

It breaks my heart, thinking he could've had more time if he'd faced it head-on. But he didn't want us to see him weak, didn't want us to worry. And sometimes that strength we try to hold onto can be the very thing that breaks us.

Reunited With My Mom

But the real mess hit when I had to deal with my mom. See, I hadn't seen her in forever, but my grandma had just had a stroke, and I was in New Orleans to get my mom to visit her. I went to this house where they had my mom locked up, and it was crazy. These girls, the owners of the facility, had bars up, and my mom's trapped inside. Nobody's there, and I had to call the cops just to get in. When they showed up, those girls pulled up too, talking big, saying my mom couldn't go anywhere. I was like, "Oh, she's coming with me."

My mom was in bad shape. Feet swollen, barely able to walk, and she wasn't getting the care she needed. Independent living my ass. I knew something was shady. So I hit up my Tee Tee who worked for the news to investigate. When she looked into it, she dropped a bombshell: that house? It wasn't some official care facility. They had my mom's house in *her* name and were renting out rooms to random men. And worse, they were touching her. The whole thing made me sick to my stomach.

The cops were knocking hard, like they weren't playing around. They said, "If y'all don't open this door, 'cause this is Pat's house, we're about to open it for you." I was ready to turn off my camera and go off on them. They had no clue how close they were to catching these hands. Finally, my mom is able to come out, and as she's sitting in the car, I'm telling her, "Pat, come get your clothes." She's like, "I don't wanna get out," and that's the first time I ever heard my mama sound scared. I was like, "What's the problem? Are you scared of these people?" That's when she dropped it on me, told me that the men in that house had been touching her.

I lost it. "They got *men* in here?!" I couldn't believe it—this whole house was in my mama's name, and they're out here renting rooms to random dudes? Leaving her here to fend for herself? I hadn't seen my mama in years, and now, here I am, back for my son's father's funeral, barely holding it together, and I gotta save my mama too? My grandma was already fighting for her life, and now I'm out here making sure my mama gets out of this mess. There was no way I was leaving her here, no way.

Turns out, the state had her in this independent living program, where she was supposed to get 24-hour care. But they'd been neglecting her, big time. So now I'm fighting tooth and nail to get her out of there, I said, "I'm taking her to Atlanta with me. That's all I got right now." My mama made it clear—she wasn't coming back. She said it herself.

I took her straight to the hospital. They checked her over real good, and my mama—she filed her own report. She spoke up, used her own voice, told the cops everything about how she'd been assaulted. I wasn't even in the room when she did it. The police took her statement, and she signed her name herself. But here's the kicker—they never called me back. Nothing. Not a word about that assault charge my mama put on them. And it wasn't even me filing it—it was *her* standing up for herself.

They hit that house with nine charges of neglect, but what did they do? They just fined them. That's it. No accountability, no checking on my mama's well-being, no follow-up. And here I am, clueless about her condition, what meds she's on, I knew nothing. I had to figure it all out on my own, flying my mama back and forth to Atlanta, scrambling to get her meds, and fighting just to get them to release her money to me. It took six whole months before I could access her funds to take care of her. Meanwhile, I'm losing my house, going through a divorce, but still making sure my mama has what she needs—new clothes, flowers, anything to make her feel loved, even though I barely had the strength to keep myself going.

And just when I thought things couldn't get worse, I had to head to New Orleans to help with my grandma's funeral. I flew me and my mama out there, on the day of my grandmother's service, still trying to figure out how to move my furniture and hold it together. It felt like the world was crumbling around me, but I wasn't about to let them break me. I had to stay strong—for my mama, for my family.

Chapter 6

CRUMBLING OUT OF CONTROL

wasn't done fighting though. I moved my mom with me to Atlanta, but I still had so much going on. By this time I was newly married to a new guy that I met. My marriage was falling apart. I was losing my home, but I had to hold it together for her. I gave her everything I had—new clothes, love, care— while my life was crumbling.

Then, in the middle of it all, my grandma passed. My mom, out of nowhere, decided she wanted to go to the funeral in New Orleans. I didn't want to go at all, but she insisted. So there we were, rushing through the airport. I hadn't even dressed my mom properly, so I warned her, "Don't embarrass me by saying you ain't got no underwear on this plane." We were a mess, but we made it.

The funeral from hell

When we got to the funeral, it was cold. No one cared. My family acted like strangers. My mom walked up to her mama's casket, just shaking her, saying, "Get up." It was heartbreaking. It felt like a final goodbye, but it also felt like she never really understood what was happening. Maybe that was her closure, but for me? It just left a whole lot of questions.

So, imagine this: the pastor is standing there, just casually saying, "This lady's been on this earth for ninety-four years, and ain't nobody got nothing nice to say." Like, whoa. That statement hits like a gut punch. The whole room is buzzing, but it's this awkward, bitter kind of vibe.

There's these sisters—let's call them Sister One, Sister Two, and Sister Three—sitting there, their faces telling a story without saying a word. And then, out of nowhere, Sister Two jumps up and walks out of the funeral. Right before the pastor's words hit. Like, what's going on there? The kids and grandkids are sitting around looking lost, and nobody's crying. Mind you, this woman—grandma—was a major part of their lives. Yet here they are, cold, almost numb. It's like the grief is wrapped up in so much unresolved drama that nobody knows how to process it.

And then there's you, in this daze. You're not dressed for the occasion—still in pajamas, hair wild—like you didn't even have time to pull yourself together because life has been throwing punches non-stop. People are whispering, side-eyeing, thinking something's wrong with you. Like, "Is she on something?" But they don't know what's really going on. You just buried your son's father, and now you're burying your grandma too. You finally have custody of your mom and facing homelessness. The weight of that alone is enough to knock anyone out. Not to mention the divorce that was completely stressing me out too!

But in the middle of all this chaos, I found a weird kind of peace. You stand up, speak some words about your grandma, and you're like, "I'm good. I don't need to cry. I've made my peace with her." Meanwhile, the rest of the family is still lost in their own drama, acting like you don't even exist, treating the funeral like it's nothing but a financial headache.

And speaking of headaches—Sister Three from Texas refuses to chip in because, you know, "gas money." Sister Two, she's not giving a dime either because, in her mind, their mother should have planned her own funeral in advance. The bitterness is so thick you can cut it with a knife. And then there's you, stepping up when no one else would, throwing down $500 to help that my friend Carla had just donated to help me find a new home, even though you also find out that your house just caught on fire in the middle of all this madness.

Everything is happening all at once—funeral drama, family feuds, literal fires—and somehow, you're in the eye of the storm, trying to hold it all together.

Everything was happening at once. I'm down in Florida, right? Kitchen caught on fire, the house in shambles, and now I'm thinking, "I need my $500 back 'cause me and mama are gonna need a place to stay." Meanwhile, nobody's even thinking about where we're gonna live afterwards. My house is burning up, no place to stay, no car. Sister number two snatched the paperwork for the car, so my grandma didn't even get to sign it. Sis pulled a fast one, and after we buried my grandma, she finally admitted she had the papers all along. Shady. That's right, that car that my grandmother co-signed for me, my shady auntie hid the paperwork so that she couldn't sign them. Now I have to return the car too.

Now I'm beefing with sister number two 'cause she's been on some grimy stuff. My mama sees her at the funeral, and she's crazy about sister number two. They look just alike. But sis walks straight past her like she doesn't even exist. I told my mama, "Stop speaking to these people, just stop." After the service, me and mama dipped out. I had to head back to Florida, I left the U-Haul with all our stuff just sitting there. So, I pulled up to the U-Haul lot and told the people they could have everything in that truck. That's how done I was with it all.

Homeless and nowhere to go…again

I had struggled through homelessness multiple times in my life. It now felt like an old, unwelcome friend. This time, though, I was determined to slam the door in its face for good.

My oldest daughter came down, and we started driving back to New Orleans, but let me tell you what really set me off before this happened—my own daughter had me thrown in jail. She told everybody I was losing it, going through my divorce, losing my grandma and just losing my mind. So what do they do? They show up, slap a straight jacket on me, and lock me up. All this happened 'cause I was evicting my daughter and her girlfriend out of my house in Atlanta. They weren't paying the bills, and when I got back, I'm looking at stacks of unpaid bills. I'm like, "Hold up, if I let y'all stay here for free, at least keep up with the bills." But nope. House almost gone, and I gotta take it back.

So I said, "Everybody gotta roll up outta here." My daughter then turns around and tells her little friend that she doesn't have to leave. Now, let me tell you about this friend—it's my best friend's daughter. Yeah, you heard that right. So I called my best friend, like, "Look, I need you to come get your daughter. She's not about to get slick with me in my own house. Come get her, or it's gonna be a problem." My friend was like, "Do what you gotta do."

So I go outside, flat out this girl's tires, and my daughter's standing there recording the whole thing. They called the cops on me and had me arrested for vandalism—on *my own property*!

I hadn't spoken to my daughter in about six months, It was wild. I moved in with my auntie—the one I told you we're tight with. I brought my mama along, thinking that'd help. Auntie was cool with it, so I was paying her $700 a month. I was working as a receptionist for the state, so I figured she could keep my mama while I was at work and still pay her. But here's the kicker: they weren't giving me my mama's income, so I was trying to juggle everything—paying bills, finding us a place, and making sure mama had what she needed. I was hustling hard just to keep us afloat.

One night, things got outta control. I'm not sure what happened, maybe her meds were off, but mama flipped and hit me while I was sleeping. Auntie got scared and we ended up taking her to the hospital. I wasn't scared of mama; I knew she was struggling. They kept her for a week and found out she was suffering from thyroid issues. Her levels were all messed up, and here she was, taking all this medicine but nothing for the thyroid. It was a lot for her body to handle.

When she got home, she still wasn't right. Auntie was getting worn out, and after about five months, she told me, "Look, Trina, you can stay, but I can't handle your mama anymore." That hit me hard. Like, that's your sister! I asked, "What are you gonna do, send her back to the hospital?" My kids were outside, heated, saying they weren't coming back in if grandma was getting kicked out. They were like, "This is crazy, Ma, we're not doing this." And I'm sitting there thinking, "Where the hell am I supposed to go?"

My youngest daughter had some cash saved up, and I remembered how me and my mama cosigned for a loan back when we were planning on getting a house. So I figured maybe we could use that to make something happen. But then my auntie called the ambulance and they took mama away again. When it was time for her to be discharged, the hospital called me saying, "You gotta come get her." I was like, "I don't have anywhere to take her. I'm at my auntie's place." And they were like, "Well, if you don't pick her up, that's abandonment." I was furious. I didn't put her there; my auntie called them.

They said, "You brought her from New Orleans, so you're responsible." At that point, I was fuming. The nurse mentioned getting an advocate involved and throwing neglect charges at me and Auntie for not picking her up. Things got heated between me and Auntie, and I was feeling trapped. No credit, no cards, nothing.

Back to Atlanta we go

Then my baby girl had a bright idea—she said, "Let's just rent a U-Haul and head back to Atlanta. We got family and friends there." And that's exactly what we did. We rolled back to Atlanta, thinking maybe we could find some peace there. We stayed for about a month or two, just trying to catch our breath and figure out the next move.

My favorite cousin Kee in Atlanta hit me up, told me to come crash at her place for a bit. I figured a week wouldn't hurt, but let me tell you, it felt awkward dragging all my baggage into her house. I was a hot mess, just trying to pull myself together and find a way to get my mama back. So, after a week, I dipped and ended up at a hotel. But, that hotel bill was eating me alive.

Then my oldest daughter called. She wasn't doing so hot either, so I brought her back into the fold. We were in that hotel together, trying to figure things out. On our way back to New Orleans, she started feeling real sick—like, throwing up sick. She kept telling me, "Mom, I just don't feel good." I had been through too much; I knew mental health and physical health were tied together. So I started to panic. We were cruising down the highway, and I said, "First hospital exit I see, we're stopping."

God's grace

We pulled into a hospital in Houma, Louisiana. I was in the waiting room, praying like a madwoman. The doctor came out and hit me with the news: "Your daughter needs emergency surgery." I felt my heart drop. He said if I hadn't stopped when I did, she could've died—her appendix had ruptured, and the poison was spreading through her body. I was like, "What?" I couldn't believe it. God was clearly watching out for us, turning my daughter's pain into a wake-up call for me.

So there we were, stuck in that hospital for three days while she recovered. I slept in the ER waiting room, holding onto faith that she'd pull through. She looked at me and said, "If it wasn't for you…" We were homeless, but we had each other. We were going through it together, figuring it out as we went.

I finally got an apartment in Baton Rouge, even though it was in both our names. I thought, "Okay, I can get my mama back now that I've got a place." But it was too late. They had already placed her with an advocate after I left the hospital. I was crushed. It took me a year or two before I could visit her again. I was still trying to get on my feet, still paying for my son's college. I had to focus on myself.

Chapter 7

THE REBIRTH

Depression and anxiety were killing me slowly. From thyroid cancer, to breast cancer, to not eating solid food for 14 years. They had their hooks in me, not wanting to let me go.

At first, anxiety and depression were a constant buzzing in my ears, drowning out everything else. As years passed, it morphed into a weight on my chest, making each breath a conscious effort. It wasn't until I started healing that I realized anxiety had become my twisted version of an old friend — familiar, but no longer welcome."

I started getting into fitness, meditating, and praying. I had to find a way to heal myself. I'd gone from sleeping in a U-Haul to the hospital, and I knew I didn't want to go back to anyone for help this time. I had to feel every ounce of pain because I knew that pain would turn into purpose. How could I help someone else if I hadn't walked that road myself? So, I told myself, "I'm gonna sleep in this Uhaul if I have to."

I figured out how to get a car, and my daughter and I went back to sleeping in it. I worked temp jobs, did whatever I could to keep going. The more I pushed through, the stronger I became. Then tragedy struck: my daughter's friend got brutally murdered. Her mom had already been through hell, dealing with abuse and everything else. But after her daughter's death, I watched this woman transform into a powerhouse. She broke every curse that had been holding her back.

So I dove into prayer, into the Bible. I went to every church service I could find, doing all the right things, but still felt stuck. I was writing letters, trying to figure out if I really forgave everyone who'd hurt me. It felt like something was blocking my release.

Then I reached out to a friend who became family named Diamond—supposedly, she was the one to break curses. When Diamond showed up, I was drained. She brought her daughter, and they came into my living room and prayed for me. When Diamond's hands came off me, I felt a wave lift off my shoulders—like I was free. From that moment on, everything changed.

I dove into the Word, grew closer to God, became a member and a sisterhood of the Healing Circle. This prayer circle changed me in so many ways. My sis Keyshawn, a powerful woman of God would go live on Ingram M-F. With prayer I showed up every morning, I was hungry for God's word. We drew closer in our relationship and built a bond as sisters. Her prayers gave me strength. We would host healing events and also had feed the block meetings in areas where no one would go ..I am still well connected to the healing circle, it helped me find my spiritual connection when things were dark in my life. Now things are looking like they are coming together. I got my apartment in Baton Rouge, and became a leasing agent. I started connecting with the right people. With all that was going on in my life I still had to help my son move from Jackson State to Grambling State University, and he was worried we wouldn't be able to make it happen. But God had a plan. He told me to reach out to Coach Hugh Jackson, and when I slid into his DMs on Instagram, he responded right away. My son had been trying to get in touch for sometime. It felt like a miracle, like God was showing me that I was on the right track.

I said, "Listen, I'm sending you these videos of my son. I ain't just saying this because he's my blood. I'm saying this because he never got a fair shot in life." I needed people to see him for who he truly was—talented, driven, ready to break through. After all we had been through, I felt like it was time for something good to happen.

I began to deepen my relationship with God. I was hanging out with my family and going to my son's football games. I was believing and trusting with all my heart at this time.

The email that changed everything

Then, out of the blue, I got an email that flipped my whole world upside down. I was still deep in prayer, back in New Orleans, and asking God to connect me with the right people and open the right doors. That's when I got this email from a woman named Shaisnnon Poshe Anderson. Now Shannon known for her story and book *Stripper To Striver,* where she talks about how she went from being sexually abused as a young child and going into the adult entertainment industry at the age of 15.

She completely turned her life around and has built a successful publishing company where she has helped hundreds of people to write and publish their books.

She wanted to now do the same for t.v and help people to share their stories through media and film. She was looking for people to be on her new show, *Story to Story with Shannon.* I had to do my homework on her, and once I did, I knew that this was my shot. I prayed hard, saying, "Lord, let this woman see my story and give me a chance."

We hopped on a call, and I laid it all out there—my life, my struggles, and my dreams. A few weeks later, I followed up, and she told me to come to her studio in Atlanta, GA, to shoot the show. But here's the kicker—I had no clue how I was going to get there. My heart raced; this was what I had been praying for! Sometimes you gotta make a way out of no way when it feels like it's your moment. I didn't care how; I just knew I had to be there.

I scraped together what little I had and booked a flight. But just a day before I was set to leave, my son's best friend, who I considered my own son, tragically passed away. I was torn between going to the funeral and seizing this opportunity of a lifetime. I felt his spirit right there with me, saying, "You gotta go to Atlanta. This is your moment!" So, I followed my heart and hopped on that flight.

We shot the show on the very day of his funeral. It was heavy, but I knew he was with me. When the episode dropped, I went viral—multiple times. It was like God was saying, "See? You were right to trust me!" I couldn't hold back. I told Shannon I wanted to write a book, and even though she was diving into her new TV show, she'd built her name as a book publisher over the years. She signed me to a book deal, and look at me now! If I had never taken that leap of faith, I'd still be stuck in the same cycle.

After that, the floodgates opened. Speaking gigs, conferences, podcasts, interviews—my DMs exploded with messages from folks thanking me for sharing my story. It hit me hard—like, how is this even real? I was in tears, reflecting on all that God was doing in my life. I stayed faithful, but the biggest lesson? I was obedient!

If God did it for me, I know He can do the same for you. I always tell people, *"The Lord is my strength."* I'm hyped about this new journey ahead, and I'm so grateful to you, the reader, for taking the time to dive into my story and pick up this book. It means the world to me. Keep the faith and trust God—He's got a plan for you, too. I'm building a new relationship with my mother and still fighting to have her released. I've reunited with my brother and am also seeking justice for him. This is just the beginning!

To be continued...

Trina Dorsey Thompson

Family Matters

IN MY CHILDREN'S WORDS

Many people have asked me how my children feel about my life and my family situation. I sat my children down in my thirties and explained as best that I could. Overall, they said that they express a deep sense of understanding and compassion when reflecting on my family ties. They explained to me that they can't hold any anger or resentment toward a man they never met, my grandfather, as they have no connection to him. However, their relationship with my grandmother was filled with love. They remember her as a second mother who showed them kindness and warmth, and they miss her deeply. They hold no blame or judgment toward her, only gratitude for the love she gave them.

As for my mother, whom they never had the chance to know, they feel a sense of hope and excitement. They recognize her as their grandmother and are eagerly looking forward to the day she returns home, so they can begin building new memories and relationships together, moving forward as a family.

With a tender heart, they acknowledge the pain that I, their mother endured and the strength shown in overcoming it. They are ready to embrace this new chapter with me, filled with love, forgiveness, and the hope of rebuilding together. All of us, together.

Be sure to tune in to our new t.v show *The Real Tea With Tree, Family Matters* where we go deeper into the story as the story is still unfolding. We will discuss the twists and turns and our road to victory, breaking generational curses, while helping other families to heal as well.

Search The POP Television Network on YouTube and Roku

Or go to www.ThePopTelevisonNetwork to view episodes

How to find Trina
Instagram:@tretooblessed
TikTok: TrinaDorsey2019
Facebook: Trina Thompson

Order Merch and Tour Info
Www.TheLiesTheyToldBook.com

What is Incest?

Incest is defined as sexual contact between blood relatives—siblings, parents, children, grandparents, aunts, uncles, nieces, and nephews.

Statistics of Incest

Between 1980 and 2022, about 15% of U.S. families reported an incident of incest. Research estimates that 10-15% of the general population has had at least one encounter of an incestuous nature, yet only 20% of victims report these crimes to the authorities.

Why is Incest Considered a Crime?

- **Genetic Disorders:** Incestrual relationships can lead to severe genetic defects in offspring.

- **Family Stability:** Incest wreaks havoc on family dynamics.

- **Child Protection:** Incest is often linked to child sexual abuse, although incest laws fail to address this adequately.

- **Public Morals:** Generally, incest is viewed as unnatural and immoral.

Countless studies have delved into the chaos stemming from incest and the psychological toll it takes.

According to IncestAware.org, the fallout is akin to that experienced by survivors of other forms of sexual violence, leading to:

- **Resources** Financial instability, unemployment, and homelessness.

As you can see, incest can create a multitude of complex issues, weaving a web of emotional, psychological, and societal challenges that can have lasting repercussions for individuals and families involved.

National Suicide Prevention Hotline

Dial 988 Or visit:

www.988LifeLine.org

More Resources

www.WannaTalkAboutIt.com

If you suspect someone is the victim of incest, you can report it to the police, Child Protective Services (CPS), or the Department of Human Services

Domestic Violence hotline

1-800-799-7233

Or visit www.Thehotline.org

Ready To Write And Publish Your Book?

Mention *Trina* for discount

www.IamReadyToWrite.com (free consultation)

www.PopPublishing.com

Watch Family Matters~ Healing through family trauma

www.ThePopTelevisionNetwork.com

Get The Course That Will Help You To Finally Write That Book!

www.AuthorMastery.com

Use Promo Code Trina for discount

Made in the USA
Columbia, SC
23 November 2024

46826942R00054